a youth devotional on identity

a youth devotional on identity

Annette LaPlaca

foreword by Ash Mundae

SHAW BOOKS

an imprint of WATERBROOK PRESS

Someone Like Me

A SHAW BOOK

PUBLISHED BY WATERBROOK PRESS

2375 Telstar Drive, Suite 160

Colorado Springs, Colorado 80920

A division of Random House, Inc.

ISBN 978-0-877-88233-6

Printed in the United States of America

2002

146502721

For Angie

contents

Don't Give Up

Tell me where do you hide away
What are the secrets you keep far away
Hoping no one will see
Saving it all for a rainy day
But someday soon your heart is going to break
And God only knows your need

And when your walls come crashing down
And they take you to the ground
Don't give up now

Do you believe in miracles
Did you think faith was only natural
To someone just like me
I'm not the only one who sees you
And you were made to know that heaven's true
And today's the day you'll see

And when your world comes falling through
And you don't know what to do
Don't give up now

—JEREMY ASH, CHUCK ASH, AND JIM COOPER
recorded on the Ash Mundae album Model Citizen

foreword

During the writing and recording of our Red Hill album *Model Citizen,* my brother, Jeremy, and I were reading like crazy, sometimes three or four books at a time. I know it fueled most of the ideas behind the music we were creating. Some of the books we were reading at that time were works of fiction like *Les Misérables* and *Crime and Punishment.* But we are also huge fans of Brennan Manning and C. S. Lewis; we basically consumed most of their writing by the time the album was finished. All of that is to say that I know what a great influence reading can have.

Whether it is a novel or some spiritual work I am reading, it always does what reading is meant to do: it makes me pause and think. As simple as that sounds, it's the most important thing I can do every day. On a regular basis I need to consider the things that are important to me, who I am, what I believe, and how I can translate my convictions into everyday living.

A devotional book like this one shouldn't be a spiritual hoop we jump through; it should be a chance to be reminded of who we are and who we have yet to become. That's basically the thought that inspired the song "Model Citizen." My hope is that this book will be a chance for those who read it to connect with God in ways that make them think and that inspire them to prove by their actions that we, as children of God, can be a people of humility, compassion, unconditional love, and acceptance.

Life is about making connections—connecting first with our heavenly Father and then connecting with those around us. It's why we're here, and if this book does nothing more than help us make those connections, it will have done a world of good.

—CHUCK ASH from Ash Mundae

who are you gonna be?

These are important days in your life. You may not think about it much, but the choices you are making are telling the world tons about what's important to you. What do you wear to school? Which hobbies or interests do you pursue? Who do you hang out with? How are you handling your family relationships? What you *do* says a lot about who you *are*—inside.

But no one knows the real, inside-your-skin you except God. He's given loving attention to creating you, and he cares about your feelings and your hopes for the future. So your relationship with God can be the center point of your life—the inside strength that helps you become outwardly the person you want to be.

God's Word is the place to turn as you move ahead, making choices that will take you closer to your dreams. Focus on God—on loving and obeying him—and the unique person you are will come into clearer focus too.

who, me?

Psalm 139:13-17

Lindy pulled her jacket tight against the winter wind that blasted her when she came out the gym doors. She and Amy had yelled themselves hoarse cheering for the basketball team and then jumped up screaming when the buzzer rang—their school's team had won by three points in overtime! They pushed through the crowd of students and parents to make a run for Amy's mom's car; it was late and they still had homework to do.

As Lindy slid past an old woman in the parking lot, she met the woman's eye for just a moment. The old woman's hand reached out to touch Lindy's sleeve, and she said with a smile, "Jesus loves you, young lady!"

Lindy dashed after Amy.

An hour later, with her math assignment ready to hand in, Lindy snuggled down under her blankets in the dark. She remembered the woman outside the gym. It was an interesting possibility: Did Jesus really love her? Did he even know her?

DNA and All That Stuff

God knows Lindy all right! He's known us all since before we were born. We humans can study DNA and chromosomes and try to guess what characteristics an unborn child might have, but God knows all along. And he pays close attention too!

> You created my inmost being;
>> you knit me together in my mother's womb.
> I praise you because I am fearfully and wonderfully
>>> made;
>> your works are wonderful,
>> I know that full well.
> My frame was not hidden from you
>> when I was made in the secret place.
> When I was woven together in the depths of the earth,
>> your eyes saw my unformed body.
> All the days ordained for me
>> were written in your book
>> before one of them came to be.
> How precious to me are your thoughts, O God!
>> (Psalm 139:13-17)

Before the World Began

Jesus has been loving Lindy and the rest of us for a long, long time, and his act of love in dying on the cross made a way for us to be right with God. God has been waiting for Lindy and for us to be part of his family.

Long ago, even before he made the world, God loved us and chose us in Christ to be holy and without fault in his eyes. His unchanging plan has always been to adopt us into his own family by bringing us to himself through Jesus Christ. And this gave him great pleasure. So we praise God for the wonderful kindness he has poured out on us because we belong to his dearly loved Son. (Ephesians 1:4-6, NLT)

When did you first learn that God knew and loved you? Who told you about God's love?

Do you sometimes forget about God's love for you? What could you do to remind yourself of his love?

Doesn't it feel great that someone knew you before you were born and chose you before the world began? Think about God's wonderful love for you and thank him for it.

downstairs backward

Ephesians 2:8-10

Monica pushed her chair back from her computer after reading the latest e-mail message from her ex–best friend, Heather. She had to admit that Heather was starting to make sense.

When Heather had moved away three months earlier, it had seemed like the end of the world to them both. The girls plastered their bedroom bulletin boards with pictures of each other and mementos of the great times they'd shared: matching hot pink and purple headbands they'd bought in the fourth grade, the program from the seventh-grade play they'd starred in together, ticket stubs from the one and only rock concert they had ever attended, pictures of their eighth-grade graduation—of Heather and Monica with their arms around each other's shoulders.

Monica looked up at her bulletin board and sighed. It wasn't just geographical distance that had turned Heather into a stranger. After her family moved, Heather had made some friends who went to church. The next thing Monica knew, Heather's e-mails were filled with explanations about how Christ died to save people from eternal death and to make them friends with God. Heather pleaded with Monica to check out

Christianity for herself. She even called once, and both girls cried over the telephone in frustration.

Friend to Friend

One of Heather's e-mails to Monica went like this:

> Monica,
> All our efforts to be good and to be so perfect in school
> and our looks and everything are a waste. It doesn't get
> us anywhere. It doesn't help us know God any better.
> Don't you get it? It's like walking backward down the
> stairs when you're trying to go up! There's nothing you
> can do to earn God's love—you just have to say yes to
> it. I'm praying for you! Love always, your friend forever,
> Heather :-)

Monica had never thought much about God or what would happen after she died until Heather started sending her those e-mail messages. Thinking about eternity did make her efforts seem wasted. Suddenly she wanted to know why she was living and what she could do to make her life seem worthwhile.

Did It Happen to You?

Monica had learned from Heather that Jesus Christ was more than just a religious teacher, as she had always thought. Jesus was God in human flesh. Because he was a man, he could sympathize with people who mess up (that would be all of us). And because Jesus was divine and sinless, God accepted his death as payment for the sins of all who put their trust in him.

Monica felt like there was a lot left for her to learn about this spiritual stuff, but it made sense to her that, if God was truly loving, he would make a way for people to come to him, even if it cost him dearly.

If you already are a Christian, write about when you accepted God's gift of salvation. Thank God today for accepting you into his family.

If you have never accepted God's gift of salvation and have questions like Monica's, write out your questions here:

It is by grace you have been saved, through faith—and
this not from yourselves, it is the gift of God—not by
works, so that no one can boast. For we are God's
workmanship, created in Christ Jesus to do good
works, which God prepared in advance for us to do.
(Ephesians 2:8-10)

Don't wait to become a member of God's forever family, even if all your
questions aren't answered. Tell God that you need his salvation and that
you want to belong to him. The gift is free—you can't earn it. Just take it
and watch God work in your life!

turning point

Jeremiah 6:16

Six months earlier, everything was fine in Andrew's life—his faith, his friends, his family, his church, everything. But when his family moved out of state and he had to start all over again, things started happening fast.

His parents decided on a new church right away, and at first Andrew was happy with their choice. The youth group was large, the kids seemed nice, and lots of them went to his school. Almost immediately he realized that there was a cool group and a geek group, and he felt fortunate that he made friends quickly with the cool people. Andrew spent more time with friends from church than he ever had before, and his parents were delighted. They felt confident that Andrew was growing spiritually. So did Andrew. After all, it must please the Lord for Andrew to be in God's house so often and to hang out with his people.

A Pain in the Head—and in the Conscience

But last night he'd been at the home of one of the church families, and he and the other guys drank some beers and half a bottle of whiskey that they had found in the kitchen. His own parents didn't drink, and up till then Andrew hadn't known any Christians who did. But the guys said it was fine, and since he didn't want to be left out of the fun, he went ahead. He'd sneaked in after curfew, brushed his teeth over and over, and swallowed mouthwash to cover up the guilty smell of alcohol on his breath.

This morning's headache was a nagging reminder of last night's escapade, and Andrew couldn't help wondering what had happened to the Christian commitment that had been so easy to live by before. Suddenly things were jumbled and confused in his mind.

At the Crossroads

The people who should have been encouraging Andrew to follow Christ were the ones who were holding him back from do-or-die commitment to the Lord. Now Andrew is at a crisis point, and he could use some guidance. If you were his friend, what advice would you give Andrew?

Whatever we're going through, other followers of God have gone through something like it before. That's what makes the Bible such a great place to go for a new perspective on our situation. Here's some advice from the book of Jeremiah that Andrew—and anyone else who has to make a decision—can use:

Stand at the crossroads and look;
  ask for the ancient paths,
ask where the good way is, and walk in it,
  and you will find rest for your souls. (Jeremiah 6:16)

It's All up to You

Being a Christian means choosing, over and over. Your first and most important choice was to accept God's gift of salvation through Christ. But every day you're making choices, either in your mind or by your actions, to live for God or to live for yourself.

Whatever you do, do it all for the glory of God.
(1 Corinthians 10:31)

Be sure to fear the LORD and serve him faithfully with
all your heart; consider what great things he has done
for you. (1 Samuel 12:24)

If you are at a decision-making crossroads, ask God to help you make a choice that will honor him.

outrageous love

Psalm 100

Elizabeth turned sideways in front of the full-length mirror in her closet and sucked in her stomach as hard as she could. The fabric across the front of her red dress pulled tight. The bathroom scale didn't lie. She *had* gained five pounds since the school year started.

Elizabeth was in a bad mood—jumbo size! The biggest social event of the school year was that night, and not only had she gotten too fat for the dress she'd bought with her own money two months before, but no one had even asked her out.

"You don't need a date," her father said. "Go with your girlfriends. Not many of them were asked either."

He made sense (even for a father), and she had planned to go with Vanessa and April. But now that the night had actually arrived, she felt like crawling into a hole and never coming out. She put on her sweats, called Vanessa and April to tell them to go without her, got out her diary and a pen, and crawled under her electric blanket to wallow in self-pity.

"Fat-fat-fat!" she scrawled across the first blank page she came to. "Fat and unpopular and grouchy and unlovable!"

Singing the Blues

Elizabeth has a bad case of the blues, and it's making her exaggerate small problems into huge ones. That's a mistake many of us make. For you, the problem may not be a little extra weight. Instead, it may be a nose that you think would look right at home on a toucan's face. Or maybe it's skin that's in a constant state of breakout no matter what acne-busting product you put on it. Hey, even supermodels complain about their looks sometimes! The thing to do is to recognize that no one's perfect and to try to take a realistic attitude toward your deficiencies.

When was the last time you were in a major bad mood? What caused it?

Now, think about it. Do five extra pounds of weight make a person unlovable? Does an important night without a date make a person unlovable? Write out some healthy advice for Elizabeth's self-esteem.

Snap Out of It!

Elizabeth is a Christian, but she is acting as if she doesn't know that God loves her and that, as his child, she's a reflection of God's glory. She acts as if one whom God made and chose (Elizabeth herself!) is junk. As a child of the most high and powerful God, Elizabeth should be on top of the world.

> Shout for joy to the LORD, all the earth.
>> Worship the LORD with gladness;
>> come before him with joyful songs.
> Know that the LORD is God.
>> It is he who made us, and we are his;
>> we are his people, the sheep of his pasture.
> Enter his gates with thanksgiving
>> and his courts with praise;
>> give thanks to him and praise his name.
> For the LORD is good and his love endures forever;
>> his faithfulness continues through all generations.
>> (Psalm 100)

When life disappoints you, it helps to remember who you are to God. Thank him for his everlasting love and the privilege of serving him.

here comes the sun

2 Corinthians 4:5-6

Robert reached out from under his covers and tried to grab the hanging adjuster of the miniblinds on the window across from his bed. He leaned a little farther and—*thud!*—Robert fell out of bed and onto the pile of books and dirty clothes he had dumped on the floor the night before.

Kneeling, he grabbed the adjuster and gave it a twist. The miniblind slats all tilted downward and in an instant the room went from dim to brilliant.

Robert sat back and let the morning sunshine pour all over him. It was early for him to be awake on a Saturday, but he felt excited and content all at once. The feeling was so strange that he just couldn't sleep it away with a pillow over his head.

He'd attended his third Bible study in a row the night before. The youth leader had explained how people were separated from God by sin and needed a way back to God. Suddenly, it felt like someone had switched a light on in Robert's head: Jesus died to make things right between him and God!

After the group time, Robert had talked to the youth leader and they had prayed together. Robert had invited into his life the God who made the whole world, accepting the sacrifice of his Son, Jesus Christ.

I feel new! thought Robert as he sat in the flood of sunlight. *This is the greatest!*

Let the Sun Shine In

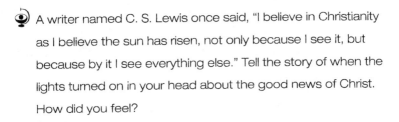 A writer named C. S. Lewis once said, "I believe in Christianity as I believe the sun has risen, not only because I see it, but because by it I see everything else." Tell the story of when the lights turned on in your head about the good news of Christ. How did you feel?

The theme of light goes right back to the first page of the Bible. Writing to some of his Christian converts, the apostle Paul had this to say:

> We do not preach ourselves, but Jesus Christ as Lord,
> and ourselves as your servants for Jesus' sake. For God,
> who said, "Let light shine out of darkness," made his
> light shine in our hearts to give us the light of the
> knowledge of the glory of God in the face of Christ.
> (2 Corinthians 4:5-6)

Life Through 3-D Glasses

Suddenly life seemed different to Robert. Accepting Christ was like putting on 3-D glasses: It changed the colors and dimensions of everything—his home and family, school, his friends, and life in the world.

When you gave your life to God, what seemed different to you?

Do you detect some differences between the way you look at the world now and the way your friends who don't know Jesus look at the world? Write down one or two of the differences you can think of.

Thank God for the gift of life with his Holy Spirit. Thank him for a new way of seeing.

why be normal?

1 Peter 1:14-16; 2:9

Valerie dipped a French fry into her chocolate shake, then popped it into her mouth.

"Disgusting!" said her sister Amanda, making a face. "You've been doing that since you were two years old. When are you going to grow up and eat ketchup like normal people?"

"Why be normal?" asked Valerie, laughing.

Amanda smiled too. She and Val had been saying "Why be normal?" to each other for years.

When Val's friends criticized her for spending her Saturdays visiting old folks at the retirement center instead of going with them to the shopping mall, Amanda told her, "Who cares what they say? Why be normal, anyway?"

When Amanda felt pressured by the other girls on the volleyball team to go to a party where there was going to be lots of drinking, Val encouraged her not to feel bad about being different: "Why be normal?"

And when friends at a slumber party teased them that they were probably the only girls in school who hadn't "done it," Val and Amanda laughed and said, "Why be normal?"

Who Makes the Rules?

Who makes the rules for "normal," anyway? Just because "everybody" is doing something doesn't make it right or wise. When Val and Amanda became members of God's family, they accepted a new standard for "normal"—a standard of holiness.

> As obedient children, do not conform to the evil desires
> you had when you lived in ignorance. But just as he
> who called you is holy, so be holy in all you do; for it is
> written: "Be holy, because I am holy."…
>
> You are a chosen people, a royal priesthood, a holy
> nation, a people belonging to God, that you may
> declare the praises of him who called you out of dark-
> ness into his wonderful light. (1 Peter 1:14-16; 2:9)

We've Got Each Other

Val and Amanda are lucky to have each other's support in standing firm in what they believe. Val and Amanda have what the Bible calls "fellowship." In a "fellowship" type of relationship, Christians keep each other faithful to God and help each other through the tough times.

> As iron sharpens iron, a friend sharpens a friend.
> (Proverbs 27:17, NLT)

Two are better than one,

    because they have a good return for their work:

If one falls down,

    his friend can help him up.

But pity the man who falls

    and has no one to help him up!

        (Ecclesiastes 4:9-10)

Do you have a "fellowship" type of friendship? If so, write your friend's name here:

How do you "sharpen" each other? How do you "help each other up"?

What steps can you take immediately to start offering more of this "sharpening" and "helping up" to other Christians?

Thank God for your friends. If you haven't got a friend to be "abnormal" with, ask God for someone to encourage you and help you up when you need it. Ask God to help you live by *his* standard for "normal."

happy—on purpose!

Psalm 16:11

It was driving Karyn nuts! Nothing kept her friend Stephanie from smiling, not even a pop quiz. One weekend Stephanie's boyfriend dumped her, and on Monday there she was—smiling! Stephanie even managed to laugh when she lost a school election or got a D on a history paper.

Karyn knew that Stephanie didn't have a dad, that her mother worked full-time, and that Stephanie stocked shelves at the grocery store. She worked hard to keep up with her job, her schoolwork, and her chores at home. Some days Stephanie looked exhausted, but she always seemed cheerful.

There didn't seem to be much connection between Stephanie's circumstances and her mood. What could be the reason for Stephanie's unfailing happiness?

You Asked for It

During homeroom, Karyn watched Stephanie out of the corner of her eye. Eventually, she couldn't stand it anymore. She finally asked Stephanie the secret of her smile.

"I used to be a grump," said Stephanie, "but now I'm happy on purpose!"

Stephanie told Karyn that she was a Christian. Knowing that Jesus loved her and that she was going to live forever with him filled her with joy. She showed Karyn this scripture:

> You have made known to me the path of life;
>> you will fill me with joy in your presence,
>> with eternal pleasures at your right hand.
>> (Psalm 16:11)

Then Stephanie explained that she actually disciplined herself to be cheerful "because God said to be!"

> Be happy...while you are young,
>> and let your heart give you joy in the days of your
>>> youth.
> Follow the ways of your heart
>> and whatever your eyes see,
> but know that for all these things
>> God will bring you to judgment. (Ecclesiastes 11:9)

What's Your JQ ("Joy Quotient")?

Nobody can be cheerful every minute. That would be impossible in the world where we live. But God wants and expects his children to find great joy in loving and serving him and in experiencing the wonderful gifts he gives us.

Think of the most cheerful person you know. Why is that person so happy? Are the reasons temporary or eternal? Is she in love and on cloud nine? Did his parents just promise him a sports car for his sixteenth birthday? Or is that person a Christian who finds joy in living for Christ? Tell about him or her.

What about you? What's your "Joy Quotient"? Have you ever felt full of joy from the Lord? Have you ever disciplined yourself to be happy? Tell about your joy experiences.

If you find it hard to be joyful, ask God to fill you with supernatural joy. Look for his goodness and everyday gifts to you. If it helps, start a "Joy Journal" and write down three or four reasons to be glad (unexpected blessings, answers to prayer, miracles) every night before you go to bed. The rise in your JQ might surprise you!

prison or paradise?

2 Corinthians 4:3-4

"Hey, Nate, did you see that movie on cable last night? You know, the one with the creature that had ten claws on each hand." Joshua contorted his face into a monsterlike grimace. Nathan had to laugh.

"Sorry, Josh, I missed that one. I had Bible study last night." Nathan Cooper pulled his geometry and biology textbooks and his dirty gym clothes out of his locker and stuffed them into his backpack.

"*Bible* study? What a waste! What kind of a wimp are you anyway, Cooper?" Joshua circled around Nathan in an exaggerated, prancing walk.

"I like it," Nathan said.

"Hey, guys!" Joshua yelled. "Natie-poo here stays at home like a good little boy and *reads the Bible!*"

Embarrassed and angry, Nathan managed to keep his mouth shut. He just shook his head, picked up his backpack, and headed for the exit.

Two Ways of Seeing

That wasn't the first time Joshua or others had made fun of Nathan's commitment to God. Sometimes they called him "preacher boy." It didn't usually bother Nathan much because they generally treated him pretty fairly. But Nathan couldn't help wondering how something so wonderful to him could seem so ridiculous to the guys at school.

Have you ever felt frustrated because a friend of yours completely misunderstood your faith? Tell about the experience. Did that friend ever come to understand?

Take the Blindfold Off!

It's not that Nathan's friends are dense. But the Bible says that they are blinded by the god of this age (Satan) to the true nature of Christianity:

> If our gospel is veiled, it is veiled to those who are perishing. The god of this age has blinded the minds of unbelievers, so that they cannot see the light of the gospel of the glory of Christ, who is the image of God. (2 Corinthians 4:3-4)

To Joshua and the other guys, Christianity is a complicated system of no-nos—just a bunch of rules to ruin their fun. They can't seem to "see"

Nathan's gladness in having a relationship with God, his contentment in having a reason to live. What seems like a prison to Nathan's friends is really true freedom and a chance to participate in God's glory.

> The Lord is the Spirit, and where the Spirit of the Lord is, there is freedom. And we, who with unveiled faces all reflect the Lord's glory, are being transformed into his likeness with ever-increasing glory, which comes from the Lord, who is the Spirit. (2 Corinthians 3:17-18)

In what ways do you experience freedom because you are a Christian?

Praise God for freedom of life with the Holy Spirit. Ask him to help you reflect his glory more and more. Pray today for the friend you remembered earlier. Pray that your friend's blindfold will be removed so that the truth of Christ's love will be visible.

inside the oddball

Matthew 5:46-48

Cheryl bit her lip, shook off her nervous feeling of dread, and decided to go the extra mile. "Want to go shopping this weekend, Melissa?"

Melissa stared at Cheryl. *What does she want with me?* she wondered, searching Cheryl's face for a glimmer of laughter so that she would know it was just another cruel joke.

But Cheryl's face was earnest. "I mean it. I want to buy a new pair of jeans, and my sister is going out of town this weekend. I usually go shopping with her."

Melissa was plain and unpopular, a loner who rarely talked to others unless she had to. She was the school oddball. She couldn't believe that gorgeous, popular Cheryl was paying attention to her, but she agreed to go along for the ride.

Not So Bad

While they were shopping on Saturday, Cheryl bought her jeans and talked Melissa into buying a whole new outfit. Much to Melissa's surprise, she discovered that underneath the good looks and fun personality, Cheryl was just normal—and nice. And much to Cheryl's surprise, underneath Melissa's shyness and ordinary clothes, she was funny and smart—and nice.

When they came out of the mall and headed for Cheryl's mom's car, Cheryl said, "Come over to my house. I'll do your makeup, and maybe you can stay for dinner."

Melissa wanted to pinch herself to make sure she wasn't dreaming!

Clue to the Mystery

When the telephone rang with a call for Cheryl, Melissa had a few minutes alone in Cheryl's room. She looked at the many pictures on the wall of Cheryl with her friends and family. This made her wonder again why Cheryl was being so nice to her. Then Melissa saw an open book on the table by Cheryl's bed and went to check it out.

Melissa's jaw dropped open from shock—it was a Bible. The worn-out book was open, and some passages had been marked with a yellow highlighter. Melissa read some of it:

> If you love only those who love you, what good is that?
> Even corrupt tax collectors do that much. If you are
> kind only to your friends, how are you different from
> anyone else? Even pagans do that. But you are to be
> perfect, even as your Father in heaven is perfect.
> (Matthew 5:46-48, NLT)

Cheryl's offer of friendship has something to do with this book, Melissa decided. *One of these days, I'll ask her.*

Out on a Limb

🌀 Have you ever gone out on a limb for God? Did it have something to do with another person? Tell about your experience.

🌀 The Bible teaches us that, although people look at the outward appearance, God sees the heart (1 Samuel 16:7). How good are your spiritual "eyes"? Do you try to see people the way God does?

God wants us to love others—the next most important thing to loving him (Matthew 22:37-40). Loving other people is one way you can show God that you love him.

> Dear friends, let us love one another, for love comes
> from God. Everyone who loves has been born of God
> and knows God. Whoever does not love does not know
> God, because God is love. This is how God showed his

love among us: He sent his one and only Son into the world that we might live through him.... Dear friends, since God so loved us, we also ought to love one another. No one has ever seen God; but if we love one another, God lives in us and his love is made complete in us. (1 John 4:7-12)

Think for a while about who the oddballs are in your school and how you could befriend them. Ask God to help you obey his love command.

good guys and bad guys

Luke 18:10-14

When four guys in black trench coats stalked over to Jake's lunch table in the school cafeteria and dropped their trays with a loud clatter, Jake got up to find "decent" company to sit with.

When his Spanish teacher assigned him "Smelly Sarah" Sanders for his dialogue partner, Jake politely asked to be reassigned.

When Jake saw the school "burnouts" entering the stadium, he decided to skip the football game and go home.

So on Sunday morning when his youth leader asked, "Is it hard to live for Christ in your school?" Jake leaned back and smiled. *It's a piece of cake!* he thought. *You just separate the bad guys from the good guys and stay away from the bad guys.*

Not So Fast, Jake!

Jake has a serious attitude problem, according to the story Jesus told about a Pharisee and a tax collector. In Jesus' day, Pharisees were known as strict religious leaders, so everyone was sure that God approved of them. They were the "good guys." Tax collectors had a well-deserved reputation for taking advantage of taxpayers. They were some of the "bad guys" of that time.

> Two men went up to the temple to pray, one a Pharisee and the other a tax collector. The Pharisee stood up and prayed about himself: "God, I thank you that I am not like other men—robbers, evildoers, adulterers—or even like this tax collector. I fast twice a week and give a tenth of all I get."
>
> But the tax collector stood at a distance. He would not even look up to heaven, but beat his breast and said, "God, have mercy on me, a sinner."
>
> I tell you that this man, rather than the other, went home justified before God. For everyone who exalts himself will be humbled, and he who humbles himself will be exalted. (Luke 18:10-14)

Write about a time when you felt "better" than another person. What were the circumstances?

Write about a time when you saw yourself and your sins clearly and realized how they looked to God. (Maybe it was the day you accepted God's forgiveness in Christ.)

Not "Us" Versus "Them"

The Bible tells us that every single person is a sinner, that all of us are equal in our need for God's grace and forgiveness.

> There is no one righteous, not even one;
>> there is no one who understands,
>> no one who seeks God.
> All have turned away,
>> they have together become worthless;
> there is no one who does good,
>> not even one. (Romans 3:10-12)

God lovingly provided salvation for sinners, and he wants everyone to be saved. Ask God to give you a spirit of love toward those who haven't yet accepted his salvation.

God demonstrates his own love for us in this: While we
were still sinners, Christ died for us. (Romans 5:8)

He is patient with you, not wanting anyone to perish,
but everyone to come to repentance. (2 Peter 3:9)

Are there certain types of people you tend to think are "beneath"
you? If so, ask God to give you his perspective on those people—and on
yourself.

a shelter from the wind

Proverbs 12:25

Jennifer raced out the door just in time to see the back end of her bus turning the corner, way up the street. She'd missed it! And all because Mr. Carothers, her geometry teacher, had kept her after school—the jerk! She dropped her load of books onto a bench and plunked herself down beside them. She'd be late to work—again!

A car horn beeped. Jennifer looked up to see popular Simone Phillips across the street in a blue car, waving at her. "I've got my mom's car," she shouted. "Do you need a ride?"

When Jennifer had settled into the passenger seat of the car, Simone said, "You look really stressed out. Is everything okay?"

Since she and Simone hadn't been good friends since middle school, Jennifer was surprised by the question. She looked to see if Simone was just making conversation or if she really wanted to know. Simone looked kind and open and seemed friendly in a serious way. The next thing Jennifer knew, tears were falling as she spilled the details of her parents' divorce, the family's financial problems, her new job, and her trouble with geometry.

An Anxious Heart and a Kind Word

Jennifer had an anxious heart. Simone's kind words made all the difference to her.

> Worry weighs a person down; an encouraging word
> cheers a person up. (Proverbs 12:25, NLT)

Do you recall a time that an encouraging word cheered you up? Describe the situation.

Simone knew that Jennifer needed to talk. How did she get Jennifer to open up so quickly? Simone is naturally a sensitive person; she's good at picking up clues and cues about others. But because she's a Christian, she works at it too—she makes a point of being caring. For her, people are a day-to-day ministry. She wants to lift people up.

> Each…will be like a shelter from the wind
>   and a refuge from the storm,
> like streams of water in the desert
>   and the shadow of a great rock in a thirsty land.
>   (Isaiah 32:2)

Weird Ministry

When you think of ministry, do you think of visiting people in an old folks' home, being a "big brother" or "big sister," or doing evangelistic work? Of course, all those *are* ways to minister. But how you treat the people you meet—your boss, a teacher, your parents, your next-door neighbor, your Great-aunt Matilda—is also a ministry. You already know from experience that the world is full of angry and hurting people. You can be an influence for joy and encouragement in the world around you.

Write the names of four people you will see this week.

What are some ways you can be "a shelter from the wind" or "streams of water" for these people?

Ask God to help you be an encourager this week.

speak up!

Proverbs 31:8-9

Samantha is pretty—there's no doubt about it. And she is lively and creative. She can make a boring bus trip into "Wacky Wildness on Wheels" or turn a dismal, rained-out youth group picnic from a flop into "Fun Without Sun." It's no big surprise that she's popular.

Now, you may be thinking, *Great! I'll bet that Samantha's a stuck-up jerk!* But if so, you're wrong. All things considered, she's a nice girl with lots of talents who loves the Lord. In fact, she knows who to thank for her gift of gab and her ability to enjoy people and activities—God!

Different

One of Samantha's biggest challenges is to remember that not everybody feels right at home in a group, that not everybody feels accepted or that they "fit."

Two months ago, a girl named Emily started coming to youth group activities at Samantha's church. She was quiet and shy in a way that made it hard for others to welcome her. Samantha guessed that her family probably didn't have as much money as most of the other families in their church. Emily came from a city more than a thousand miles from her new hometown, and everything about her seemed to shout, "Different!" Nobody really liked her much, not even Samantha, who usually liked everybody.

When the sign-up sheet for winter retreat was passed around in Sunday school, everyone was encouraged to sign up in groups of four to be assigned to cabins. Samantha could see two or three other girls signaling to her from across the room, but Emily's downcast eyes nagged at Samantha's spirit. Samantha kept remembering a verse she'd read the morning before:

> Speak up for those who cannot speak for themselves,
>> for the rights of all who are destitute.
> Speak up and judge fairly;
>> defend the rights of the poor and needy.
>> (Proverbs 31:8-9)

Sticking Your Neck out—for Love

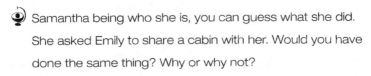 Samantha being who she is, you can guess what she did. She asked Emily to share a cabin with her. Would you have done the same thing? Why or why not?

Have you ever stuck your neck out for someone like Emily?
How did it work out? Afterward, did you feel good about your
choice? Write about the experience here.

The best example of selflessness we could ever have is Jesus Christ.

> Do nothing out of selfish ambition or vain conceit, but
> in humility consider others better than yourselves. Each
> of you should look not only to your own interests, but
> also to the interests of others.
> Your attitude should be the same as that of Christ
> Jesus:
>
> > Who, being in very nature God,
> > > did not consider equality with God something to
> > > be grasped,
> > but made himself nothing,
> > > taking the very nature of a servant,
> > > being made in human likeness.

And being found in appearance as a man,
    he humbled himself
    and became obedient to death—even death on a
        cross! (Philippians 2:3-8)

 What are some qualities of Christ that you can incorporate
into your own life to make you a better servant?

Ask God to make you more and more like his Son in looking after the
interests of others.

king of the wimps

John 15:18-19,21

Christopher Taylor dipped a scrub brush into some sudsy water and started scrubbing the bright red letters off the front of his gym locker. The disappearing words seemed to mock him: "GRANDMA TAYLOR," "BIBLE BANGER," "KING OF THE WIMPS."

His coach had met him at his locker, shaking his head sympathetically and saying, "There's no way to know who did it, Christopher, so I'm going to have to hold you responsible. I'll get the cleaning supplies, but I expect to see you here right after school."

Christopher knew who did it, though. At least, he could guess. Two weeks before, in English class, he'd ended up defending his belief in God in front of the whole class. He hadn't planned to say so much, but when the teacher started talking as if believing in God was ridiculous, he just had to speak up. Four of the guys in that class were also in his gym class, and they'd spent the past two weeks experimenting with illegal tackles during phys ed. Christopher knew they were out to get him, trying to make him angry enough to do what they would do: swear or hit back. So far, with God's help, Christopher had remained cool.

The graffiti on his locker was pretty discouraging. *But okay, Lord,* Christopher prayed while he scrubbed, *I'll even be king of the wimps for you.*

Out of This World

Three cheers and a slap on the back for Christopher Taylor! In God's eyes, Christopher is far from being king of the wimps; he's a hero!

Shortly before his death at the hands of his enemies, Jesus tried to prepare his disciples for the mistreatment that they, too, were in for. He told them:

> If the world hates you, keep in mind that it hated me
> first. If you belonged to the world, it would love you as
> its own. As it is, you do not belong to the world, but I
> have chosen you out of the world. That is why the
> world hates you.… They will treat you this way because
> of my name, for they do not know the One who sent
> me. (John 15:18-19,21)

Christianity is not for wimps. Jesus knew it and told his disciples not to be surprised when the world rejected them, persecuted them, and even killed many of them. God knows it's hard to be chosen "out of the world" and yet live right in it. But that's what we're called to do.

Muscle Building

To live courageously for Christ takes maturity. Think of maturity as having big spiritual muscles. Christopher's troubles with his English teacher and the guys in his phys ed class are like muscle-building exercises for his spiritual maturity.

What experiences have you had that were spiritual muscle builders? Write about them here.

What are some situations in your life right now that are tough for you because you are a Christian? How can you work through those situations in a godly way?

Consider it pure joy…whenever you face trials of many
kinds, because you know that the testing of your faith
develops perseverance. Perseverance must finish its work
so that you may be mature and complete, not lacking
anything. (James 1:2-4)

It's difficult to think of hard experiences as "pure joy," but that's what God
wants us to do. Pray that perseverance will finish its work in you "so that
you may be mature and complete."

burnout blues

Matthew 11:28-29

Maddie dumped the contents of her tote bag onto her bedspread along with all the other stuff that had accumulated there. The notes she'd taken as secretary for the Youth Group Leadership Team meeting slid off the other side of the bed and down beside the wall. She'd have to retrieve them later so she could type them up and print out copies for next month's meeting.

She grabbed a pink envelope and read the back of it: "Green pepper, garlic, ground beef, onion…" These were items she needed for home economics class—tomorrow! Oh well, she could pick them up on her way to school in the morning. And the letter in the pink envelope from her friend Marsha—she'd answer that tomorrow, too.

Her Bible was there among her textbooks for school. She'd taken it along, hoping for a spare ten minutes sometime during the day in which to read a few verses. It hadn't happened.

And there was her biology book. Oh no! That homework was due first period tomorrow morning.

Maddie glanced at the bright red numbers on the digital clock by her bed: 10:45 P.M. She picked up the clock and set the alarm for 6:00 A.M., knowing she'd need time to iron clothes and fuss with her hair in the morning. Tomorrow were the tryouts for the school musical.

The last thing Maddie thought before she fell asleep on her half-finished biology assignment was *If only there were more hours in the day...*

Give Me a Break!

Many things interest Maddie, and sometimes her enthusiasm for new experiences runs away with her. She has high standards for "getting things done" and "being involved." But right now Maddie needs a vacation—Maddie needs rest.

 Are you like Maddie? Can you think of a time (maybe right now) when you were so busy that you didn't have time to breathe? What were the activities that kept you so busy?

Were those activities very important, sort of important, or not very important? Look at your list of activities and rate them.

A Place of Rest

When Jesus talked about giving those he loves a full life (see John 10:10), he didn't necessarily mean "a life full of activities." Sometimes you will have more responsibilities than seems fair, and you will often have to work very hard. But Jesus intended his followers to find a place of rest in him. He said,

> Come to me, all you who are weary and burdened, and I will give you rest. Take my yoke upon you and learn from me, for I am gentle and humble in heart, and you will find rest for your souls. For my yoke is easy and my burden is light. (Matthew 11:28-29)

I wonder if Maddie ever has time to feel excited about her ministry for Christ. I wonder if Maddie has time to talk with her family members and friends. I wonder what Maddie's biology grades look like! And most of all, I wonder if Maddie misses her time in God's Word, the Bible. What do you think?

What can you do to make sure that you will take time each day to rest in Christ's love for you?

In your prayer time, thank God that he is concerned about you when you are feeling frazzled. Ask him to provide you with opportunities for real rest.

lazybones

Proverbs 6:6-11

On Friday morning, Joey yawned, stretched, and rolled away from the alarm clock's accusing face: 7:35. He'd planned to get up to clean his room before school—he was not allowed out of the house this weekend unless the room was clean, and he had big Friday-night plans with friends. Oh well, he could do it before dinner.

By the time Joey crawled out from under the covers, he had ten minutes to catch his ride to school. So instead of going down to the laundry room to look for the pile of clean clothes his mother had washed for him, he just grabbed the jeans he'd worn the day before and a rumpled shirt from the back of his desk chair. Oh well, he could dress up next week.

There was no time for the breakfast that waited on the kitchen table. Joey paid fifty cents for a candy bar from the machine at school, remembering how his wrestling coach was encouraging him to lose a few pounds and really get in shape. No time for that today. Oh well!

Five minutes into first period, he realized that he hadn't even started his history homework for next hour. So, missing the lecture his Spanish teacher was giving, he quickly scribbled some short answers to the essay questions that had been assigned. Oh well, he'd just spend some extra time reading his Spanish book over the weekend.

After school, he skipped the student council meeting he was supposed to attend because he had to get home to clean up his bedroom before dinner. By suppertime, his room was presentable—if Mom didn't inspect it too closely!

Hold Everything!

What's wrong with Joey's lifestyle? List some observations here:

Getting organized, being involved, and even getting out of bed in the morning take hard work and discipline. It might sound like something your parents would say, but it's true that God wants his people to be self-controlled and hard working.

Here are some hard words of advice for the lazy person:

> Go to the ant, you sluggard;
>> consider its ways and be wise!
> It has no commander,
>> no overseer or ruler,
> yet it stores its provisions in summer
>> and gathers its food at harvest.

How long will you lie there, you sluggard?
  When will you get up from your sleep?
A little sleep, a little slumber,
  a little folding of the hands to rest—
and poverty will come on you like a bandit.
  (Proverbs 6:6-11)

What are some things you discipline yourself to do each day?
Why do you make yourself work hard?

In what areas of life are you perhaps lazy or too disorgan-
ized? How can you change that?

Whatever you do, work at it with all your heart, as
working for the Lord, not for men, since you know

that you will receive an inheritance from the Lord as a reward. It is the Lord Christ you are serving. (Colossians 3:23-24)

God wants you to work hard for his glory. Think about how you can do that today.

dumb jock

Matthew 6:1,3-4

Bryan's dad was a former all-American athlete and a high-school coach, so Bryan had learned to say "Batter up!" and "Touchdown!" almost before he said "Mama." He played Little League baseball and soccer, and by the time he was in middle school, he was playing football, too. By high school, he was playing football in the fall and baseball in the spring and was wrestling in between. When he wasn't at a team practice, he was home shooting hoops in the driveway or playing tennis at the sports club with his brother.

Athletics were Bryan's first love, and schoolwork wasn't even a close second. Studying didn't come easy for him, but he brought home Bs and Cs and managed to stay eligible for all the sports he wanted to participate in.

So most of his friends and relatives classified him in their minds and conversations as a "jock"—sometimes even a "dumb jock."

Secret Super Servant

But Bryan has more to him than meets the eye. Like the quiet, unassuming newspaperman Clark Kent, who is really Superman, Bryan quietly commits his days and weeks to serving God and helping others. Like the time he spends at the hospital.

The first time Bryan went to the children's ward at the hospital, he visited his favorite little cousin, Amelia, who was ill for a long time. His creative weekly visits became more frequent, and Amelia and all the other kids loved his crazy antics and unexpected games and activities. He'd arrive loaded with picture books, balloons, puzzles, and even homemade videos of the great outdoors and of the kids themselves. When Amelia went home, the doctors and nurses told Bryan they would be sorry to see him go. But by then Bryan was hooked. He kept on visiting.

More than Meets the Eye

Do you ever feel labeled, like Bryan was, by teachers or students at school or by your family members? How do they see you?

Are their labels for you on target, or do you think there's more to you than meets the eye? What is that "more"?

Be careful not to do your "acts of righteousness" before men, to be seen by them. If you do, you will have no reward from your Father in heaven....

But when you give to the needy, do not let your left hand know what your right hand is doing, so that your giving may be in secret. Then your Father, who sees what is done in secret, will reward you. (Matthew 6:1,3-4)

God is not unjust; he will not forget your work and the love you have shown him as you have helped his people and continue to help them. We want each of you to show this same diligence to the very end, in order to make your hope sure. (Hebrews 6:10-11)

Don't be discouraged if the labels other people give you don't fit the real you. Remember that God knows all about your true character and your hard work in service to him.

the extra mile

Matthew 5:38-41

Ron kicked the door to his gym locker. Sure, he wasn't the most coordinated guy in school, but he didn't deserve the abuse he was getting.

Ron had just transferred from another school, and most of his new classes were going pretty well—except gym. He'd never been a great athlete, but usually he could hold his own, get through the class period, and have a fairly good time. But everything seemed different in this class. He was sure they were out to get him.

Lately they'd been playing football, and without fail, Ron was picked last, fouled most frequently, and tackled most painfully. It didn't make sense. What had he done to these guys that they should take it out on him?

After a while he started to notice that most of the guys took their cues from Michael, the biggest guy in the class. That guy was tough—his nickname was "Crowbar." He was the kind of guy you wouldn't want to meet in a dark alley at night, the kind you wished you didn't have to go to school with.

Turning a Cheek

Ron remembered some words of advice from the Bible. Jesus' disciples lived in a time when they were bullied a lot by their fellow Jews and by their Roman conquerors. They were naturally tempted to seek revenge. But Jesus told them,

> You have heard that it was said, "Eye for eye, and tooth for tooth." But I tell you, Do not resist an evil person. If someone strikes you on the right cheek, turn to him the other also. And if someone wants to sue you and take your tunic, let him have your cloak as well. If someone forces you to go one mile, go with him two miles. (Matthew 5:38-41)

Ron decided to start at the top. When the coach told Michael to put away the equipment, Ron graciously offered to do it. When Michael and his cronies deliberately fouled him, he took it silently and didn't let the coach know. When they met at the doorway to the showers, Ron politely stepped aside and waved Michael in. When they met in the halls, Ron gave Michael a cheerful "hello" and offered him a stick of gum.

The smashing, grinding, and pounding didn't stop right away, but pretty soon Michael and his buddies were staring at Ron like he was a creature from another planet. None of them had ever seen anyone react like Ron did.

And believe it or not, one day a couple of months later, Michael stopped him after class and invited Ron to his house for a pizza and video night.

Jesus' Kind of People

Ron treated Michael the way Jesus treated people when he walked the earth as a man. Once when some religious leaders picked on Jesus for hanging around with corrupt tax collectors and other sinners, Jesus stood up to them and said, "It is not the healthy who need a doctor, but the sick…. I have not come to call the righteous, but sinners" (Matthew 9:12-13). The "healthy" were the self-righteous religious leaders (at least they *thought* they were healthy); the "sick" were the sinners.

When have you gone the extra mile when it was inconvenient for you? Why did you do it?

Who is a "Michael" in your life right now—someone who is unfairly making things hard for you? Write the name here:

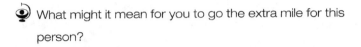 What might it mean for you to go the extra mile for this person?

God sent his Son to die for people who didn't even care about him. Thank God today for his love that went the extra mile. Ask him to make you more and more like Jesus.

your money or your life!

Matthew 6:24

Zachary slumped in the chair outside the vice principal's office. He leaned his head against the wall and drifted off to sleep. He'd just been awakened and dismissed from his English class. The teacher was fed up with his daily nap during the lecture.

Zachary was up by 4:00 A.M. every day, delivering papers on three paper routes before breakfast. By the time school began, his body was worn-out from bicycling all over town. He spent his lunch period and every free moment between classes frantically preparing something that at least *looked* like a finished homework assignment. He'd dropped the tennis team—no time to practice. He mowed lawns after school. On Saturdays he stocked shelves at the hardware store downtown. Sundays were an exercise in keeping Mom from noticing he was half-asleep in church; he totally fell asleep in Sunday school. After lunch with the family, he'd crash on his bed, and they'd have to wake him for supper.

Zachary had his heart set on making $3,500 before his sixteenth birthday, the day he'd get his driver's license and could go out and buy the used SUV he had his eye on. Zachary was a work junkie!

Stick 'Em Up!

If you were walking down a dark alley one night with your life savings in your jeans pocket (which would be pretty dumb, of course), and a man dressed in black from his ski mask to his boots jumped out from behind a Dumpster with a switchblade, saying, "Your money or your life!" what would you do?

Not being a two-hundred-pound macho he-man who enjoys flirting with danger, I'd hand over my wallet and offer the robber my watch, too. There's no question—of course I value my life more than money!

Actions Speak Loudest

Given the same holdup situation, Zachary would probably do like me— give up the cash. (After all, he's a work junkie, but he's not crazy.) And if you asked him, he would tell you that that he values his life more than his money. But what do his actions say? Zachary's life is consumed with moneymaking to the exclusion of friends, schoolwork, family life, fellowship, and worship.

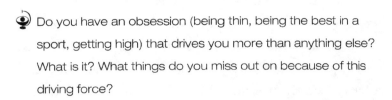 Do you have an obsession (being thin, being the best in a sport, getting high) that drives you more than anything else? What is it? What things do you miss out on because of this driving force?

Two Masters

In the first century A.D., when Jesus was alive, there were no SUVs on the market. Maybe if Zachary were living at that time he would have been saving up to buy a used mule! But there has always been a danger in becoming too attached to money and the things it can buy. Jesus had something to say about that:

> No one can serve two masters. For you will hate one
> and love the other, or be devoted to one and despise the
> other. You cannot serve both God and money.
> (Matthew 6:24, NLT)

🌐 Is your pursuit of money causing problems in your relationship with God? If so, describe how.

Zachary serves two masters, and as a result, his life is a shambles. If Jesus Christ is your first love, he should be your life's great obsession. Ask him to help you get your priorities straight—with him at the top of the list!

wallowing in "what ifs"

Matthew 6:31-33

While Trey waited for Mickey and Daniel to pick him up for the dance at school, the "what ifs" started to torment him.

What if the guys were late? What if Daniel's tin can on wheels broke down before they got to the school? What if his pants and shirt weren't nice enough? What if Meg Peters wouldn't dance with him? What if Meg Peters *would* dance with him? What if his hands got sweaty or he burped from the punch? What if...? What if...?

Trey chewed on his nails, even though they were already bitten down until they sometimes bled. Finally, he nervously sat down on top of his hands—and his knees started to shake!

Worrywart Champ

Trey could win the World Worrywart Championship. He lies awake nights, worrying. When he's asleep, he dreams about failing his classes, about girls rejecting him, about his friends abandoning him. Who would imagine that Trey is actually a nice-looking, well-liked young man who does better than average in his classes? His long history of successes doesn't seem to count in his mind—he just keeps worrying.

Join the Club

 If you worry too, join the club! Everybody does sometimes. What things make you worry most right now (for example, at school, at home, at your part-time job)?

 What things worry you about the future?

Relax, You're in Good Hands

When you became God's child, he took responsibility for keeping you healthy and whole and provided for. He expects you to be a good steward of what he's given you, but you can leave the worries up to him! You couldn't be in better hands.

Do not worry, saying, "What shall we eat?" or "What shall we drink?" or "What shall we wear?" For the pagans run after all these things, and your heavenly Father knows that you need them. But seek first his kingdom and his righteousness, and all these things will be given to you as well. (Matthew 6:31-33)

My God will meet all your needs according to his glorious riches in Christ Jesus. (Philippians 4:19)

God always holds up his end of the deal. Thank him today for his faithful love and provision. Ask him to help you trust him with your worries. Memorize Philippians 4:19 for recall during your anxious moments.

keep out!

1 Timothy 6:17-19

Matthew slipped the key into the doorknob lock. The door was plastered from top to bottom with signs reading, "STAY OUT," "TOP SECRET," "BEWARE OF MAD DOG," and "ENTER AT YOUR OWN RISK." It was Matthew's closet.

What do you think he kept in there? His clothes, yes. But that's not what he was protecting so carefully. You see, Matthew's most important possessions were locked behind that door: the unbeatable Matchbox car collection that he'd been working on since he was eight; the picture (which he'd sneaked from the yearbook office) of Melissa Sanderson, the most gorgeous and unattainable babe of his school; a baseball autographed by all the Chicago Cubs; six *Playstation* magazines; a huge EMERGENCY sign he and his best friend had found next to a Dumpster behind the hospital; twenty old issues of *Spiderman* comic books; a secret stash of Doritos and Twinkies; four mushy letters from Allison, his girlfriend from eighth grade; and the journals nobody knew he kept.

Matthew's closet was his treasure trove. He tried the handle before

he went off to school. Yes, it was locked. Anything to keep his little
brother out!

Another Kind of Treasure

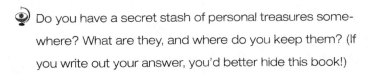 Do you have a secret stash of personal treasures some-
where? What are they, and where do you keep them? (If
you write out your answer, you'd better hide this book!)

There's a kind of treasure that can't be stored in a locked bedroom closet.
And there's a kind of wealth that people who don't follow Christ don't
know anything about.

> Command those who are rich in this present world not
> to be arrogant nor to put their hope in wealth, which is
> so uncertain, but to put their hope in God, who richly
> provides us with everything for our enjoyment. Com-
> mand them to do good, to be rich in good deeds, and
> to be generous and willing to share. In this way they
> will lay up treasure for themselves as a firm foundation
> for the coming age, so that they may take hold of the
> life that is truly life. (1 Timothy 6:17-19)

Rich in Good Deeds

In order for us to take hold of "the life that is truly life," God wants us to be rich in good deeds. Write about a time when you did something to "lay up treasure" in heaven.

Which do you tend to focus more on: laying up treasure on earth or laying up treasure in heaven? How do you feel about that?

Where Do You Keep Your Heart?

It's not wrong for Matthew to have a private place for his personal treasures—it's awesome (and I hope his brother keeps out!). But Matthew has another "treasure trove" in the storehouse of heaven that's much more important to him. Jesus said,

> Do not store up for yourselves treasures on earth, where moth and rust destroy, and where thieves break in and

steal. But store up for yourselves treasures in heaven,
where moth and rust do not destroy, and where thieves
do not break in and steal. For where your treasure is,
there your heart will be also. (Matthew 6:19-21)

The Matchbox cars, comic books, Twinkies, and old letters won't last forever, but Matthew's heart is with his treasure in heaven. Where do you
keep your heart?

treasure hunt

Proverbs 2:1-6

Joseph practically idolized his youth leader, Max. When Joseph or any of his friends were in trouble, Max was there for them with good advice and a helping hand. There were so many kids in and out of Max's apartment that Joseph and the other kids said he needed a revolving door.

One afternoon, following Max and Joseph's one-on-one discipleship meeting, Joseph shared what was on his heart. "I always hated to think I'd grow up like my dad—mad all the time and drinking a lot. I'd rather be like you, Max."

"Thanks, Joseph," said Max. "The only reason you like me, though, is that I'm trying to be like Jesus. Studying God's Word is making me a better person."

"Well, that's what I want," said Joseph with a smile.

"Okay, then. I challenge you to one month of Bible reading. Why don't you do Proverbs? Read one chapter each day, and you'll be finished this time next month. It's full of practical advice for how to be a holy man of God."

"I'll do it," said Joseph. And he did.

Foolish or Wise?

The book of Proverbs is a book of contrast and comparison—a popular writing style for the Hebrews. It falls into a category of Bible books called Wisdom Literature. In the book of Proverbs, wisdom is the hero of the story demonstrating the difference between the evil, foolish person and the righteous, wise person.

> If you accept my words
>> and store up my commands within you,
> turning your ear to wisdom
>> and applying your heart to understanding,
> and if you call out for insight
>> and cry aloud for understanding,
> and if you look for it as for silver
>> and search for it as for hidden treasure,
> then you will understand the fear of the LORD
>> and find the knowledge of God.
> For the LORD gives wisdom,
>> and from his mouth come knowledge and
>>> understanding...
> for he guards the course of the just.
>
> Wisdom will save you from the ways of wicked
>> men...
> who delight in doing wrong.
>> (Proverbs 2:1-6,8,12,14)

Go and Get It!

Wisdom is a treasure to be sought after, no matter what the cost. The author of Proverbs said, "Get wisdom!" And here's the secret to the treasure of wisdom: God is the source.

> Fear of the LORD is the beginning of wisdom. Knowledge of the Holy One results in understanding. (Proverbs 9:10, NLT)

> If any of you lacks wisdom, he should ask God, who gives generously to all without finding fault, and it will be given to him. (James 1:5)

Ask God for the treasure of wisdom right now.

know-it-all ned

1 Corinthians 8:1-3

Miss Withers sat at her desk and observed her class. The students were whispering to each other, sharing paper or pens or forbidden chewing gum. But nobody bothered Ned. He sat alone with his three perfectly pointed pencils and his flawlessly prepared notebook, complete with index tabs.

Know-It-All Ned had answered every question, word perfect every time, all through the class period. Miss Withers finally gave up any attempt at class participation (all she was getting was Ned participation) and gave a reading assignment from the textbook.

Miss Withers knew that the students didn't like Ned much. *To be perfectly honest,* she thought, *I don't like him much myself.*

Just Me, Myself, and I

People who know everything—or at least think they do—only have room for "me, myself, and I." Their thoughts, dreams, and opinions take up all the space of their lives. No wonder nobody wants to hang out with a know-it-all.

Do you know a know-it-all? (Perhaps it's you!) Describe that person's attitude.

How do you usually feel toward that person? Why?

Ned Doesn't Know Everything

The Bible says that if people think they know everything, they don't! It warns us that knowledge can make us self-important fatheads unless we keep it in perspective.

> While knowledge may make us feel important, it is love
> that really builds up the church. Anyone who claims to
> know all the answers doesn't really know very much.
> But the person who loves God is the one God knows
> and cares for. (1 Corinthians 8:1-3, NLT)

When your number-one goal is to love God, you'll focus on him. And then it's impossible to be a know-it-all, because you're focusing on the only one who really does know it all!

The Sweet Taste of Humble Pie

Ned's new youth group leader, Byron, quickly picked up on Ned's know-it-all attitude because Ned acted the same way during Bible studies as he did in school. So Byron had a talk with Ned about the importance of humility.

At Byron's suggestion, Ned has rationed himself to just one unsolicited response to the teacher per class period. It's his habit to want to talk up, but now he bites his lip. Between classes, he's trying harder to relate naturally to the other students too.

Ned's second chance should be encouraging to us. We all tend to show off now and then, in different ways, so we all could use a little humility to help us remember that we don't know everything.

The writer of Psalm 8 focused on God and was amazed that God gives us puny humans a second look. Use this psalm to praise God today.

> O LORD, our Lord, the majesty of your name fills
> the earth!
> Your glory is higher than the heavens....
> When I look at the night sky and see the work of
> your fingers—
> the moon and the stars you have set in place—
> what are mortals that you should think of us,
> mere humans that you should care for us? (Psalm
> 8:1,3-4, NLT)

sticking to it

Proverbs 8:34-36

"Tiffany," her mother called up the stairs, "Angie's here!"

Tiffany pushed aside the yellow curtains from her bedroom window and looked out into the yard. Sure enough—as sure as sunrise, home-work, and Mr. Peterman's exams—there was Angie waiting for her on the back porch.

When they'd met in the seventh grade, Tiffany had gone out of her way to be friendly to Angie, the new girl at school. She didn't know that one friendly hello would turn Angie into superglue—a friend who sticks for life. Since then they'd stuck together through thick and thin and ups and downs.

"You're lucky, you know," said Tiffany's mother to her when she came downstairs. "Not everyone would walk three blocks out of the way for a friend."

"I know," said Tiffany. "I'd hate to come down one morning and not find Angie at the door." She smiled at her mom and went out to meet the day—and Angie.

Superglue

Do you have a friend you stick to as closely as Angie sticks to
Tiffany? Put his or her name down. How many hours per
week, on average, would you say you spend with this friend?

Is there anything else you stick to as faithfully? Maybe you lift
weights or do an aerobic workout every day after school.
Maybe you discipline yourself to work on a special project. Or
maybe you set aside a half-hour each night for keeping a
journal. What activities do you stick to like superglue?

Waiting at God's Doorway

Every morning Tiffany can count on the sight of her faithful friend
Angie. In a similar way, God wants you to give him time each day. He
wants you to learn about him and to learn from him.

> Happy are those who listen to me, watching for me
> daily at my gates.... For whoever finds me finds life

and wins approval from the LORD. But those who miss
me have injured themselves. (Proverbs 8:34-36, NLT)

Studying his Word (the Bible) is one way we "watch" at God's
doorway. Talking with and listening to him in prayer is another.
How much time do you spend at God's doorway?

If you're not satisfied with the amount of time you're spending
with God, what changes do you need to make in your devotional life?

You can count on God. Be encouraged by this promise:

You will seek me and find me when you seek me with
all your heart. (Jeremiah 29:13)

Ask God to help you be faithful in spending time with him each day.

a fine line

1 Corinthians 16:13-14

Tony's mouth hung open in surprise as he listened to a young missionary tell about his adventures in South America. This guy had spent nine months as a captive of a rebel group that was hoping to raise attention and money for itself by taking an American as their hostage. The missionary had been forced to move around with the rebels from place to place, had been threatened and beaten, and had often gone without food.

The rebels had tried to convert the missionary to their particular brand of violent communism. The missionary, in turn, had preached the gospel to his captors, two of whom became believers as a result. These men escaped with the missionary just hours before he was to be executed!

Wow! thought Tony as he left the meeting. *How could I ever have thought that Christians were a bunch of wimps?*

Surprise, Surprise

Lots of people who haven't read the Bible's accounts of the adventurous Jewish keepers of the faith and the courageous New Testament church builders and martyrs have a hard time picturing Christians as tough. It's difficult to get past the stereotype of wimpy Christians.

But Christianity certainly isn't for wimps. Standing strong for Christ in today's world is a challenge that the courageous undertake with the promise of God's nearness and power.

On the Other Hand

Quiet humility and service to others are parts of the Christian's lifestyle, but so are dreaming big dreams of winning people to Christ's kingdom and fighting against the powers of darkness in the world.

Some situations call for speaking up or for direct action in order to follow Christ. Write about a time when you stood up for Christ in a difficult or public way.

Other situations call for gentler peacemaking tactics like turning the other cheek or avoiding an argument. Write about a time when you chose a seemingly "wimpy" way to follow Christ.

Two-Sided Coin

The apostle Paul was one of those courageous early Christians. He endured beatings, stonings, shipwrecks, and much more in order to take the message of Jesus to people across the Mediterranean world. Yet he also knew how to get out of the way so that people would see the Lord and not him.

Paul's words in 1 Corinthians make a great pep talk when you're feeling confused about finding the right balance between forcefulness and gentleness.

> Be on guard. Stand true to what you believe. Be coura-
> geous. Be strong. And everything you do must be done
> with love. (1 Corinthians 16:13-14, NLT)

The two aspects of strength and love are like two sides of a coin—a valuable coin! Commit yourself to serving God courageously, and let love be the standard for all your actions.

go for it!

Hebrews 13:5

When Kevin was six years old, his dad practically had to force him into riding his two-wheeler bike. Kevin was afraid of wiping out and squishing his face on the sidewalk.

When Kevin was nine, he refused to try out for the part of Abe Lincoln in his school play, even though his teacher recommended him for the part and his parents pleaded with him. Kevin was scared to get up in front of all those people—what if he made a fool of himself?

When Kevin started seventh grade, his best friend, Michael, wanted him to go out for the middle school soccer team, but Kevin wouldn't. "What if I don't make the team?" he argued.

When Kevin was a freshman in high school, all his friends on the student council and his student council advisor encouraged him to run for class president. "No way," said Kevin. "What if I lose?"

No Guts, No Glory

Because his dad forced him, Kevin eventually did experience the thrill of pumping the bike pedals until the wind whipped against his face and he was balancing with no hands. But because he is afraid of failure, Kevin missed out on opening-night jitters and the sweet sound of applause, the camaraderie and the satisfied feeling of washing off mud and sweat after a good workout, and the exhilaration of the vote count and the responsibility of representing others. Kevin is a classic case of no guts, no glory.

What challenges have you turned away from because you were afraid to fail?

What experiences or emotions do you think you missed out on because you hesitated?

Have Confidence!

We as Christians can't afford to let fear keep us from going out on a limb to serve God. We can have confidence because God has promised to be with us, to help us, and to carry us through to the end.

> Never will I leave you;
> never will I forsake you. (Hebrews 13:5)

Such confidence as this is ours through Christ before
God. Not that we are competent in ourselves to claim
anything for ourselves, but our competence comes from
God. (2 Corinthians 3:4-5)

[I am] confident of this, that he who began a good
work in you will carry it on to completion until the day
of Christ Jesus. (Philippians 1:6)

The LORD will fulfill his purpose for me;
> your love, O LORD, endures forever.
> (Psalm 138:8)

Thank God today for his presence and power. Ask him to help you to be
confident in his strength.

great expectations

Jeremiah 29:11-14

Tamika stuck the tip of her finger in her mouth. "Another paper cut!" she groaned. When it stopped bleeding, Tamika went back to filing papers in the big gray cabinets in her father's office.

She had been working after school for three weeks in her dad's television news studio, and she had hated every minute of it. She'd only said yes because Dad had come home so excited about the job. She loved him so much—she just couldn't disappoint him. But now tryouts for the spring musical were coming up, and if she got a part, it would mean long, wonderful hours of rehearsal after school. How could she tell Dad that she wanted to quit?

It wasn't just that he would be disappointed that she didn't love television the way he did. ("It's show biz, honey, in a way," Dad always said.) Dad had been dreaming big dreams for her practically since the day she was born. "You could be a director. You could even be an anchorwoman —you've got the looks and the brains! Oh, sweetheart, have I got great expectations for you!"

Parent Pressure

Tamika feels trapped by her dad's great expectations of her, even though she knows the only reason he has big dreams for her is that he loves her.

🌐 Have you ever felt pressure about your future from your mom or dad or older brothers and sisters? Or maybe from someone else? How did you feel about it? Were you able to talk to the person about it?

🌐 What advice would you give Tamika about talking with her dad? What would work at your house?

Top Secret Plans

Somebody besides Tamika's father is planning good things for her, and Tamika is learning more and more to seek God's guidance. After all, who could be better at knowing what's best for Tamika than the one who created her and holds her future in his hands?

> "I know the plans I have for you," declares the LORD,
> "plans to prosper you and not to harm you, plans to
> give you hope and a future. Then you will call upon me
> and come and pray to me, and I will listen to you. You
> will seek me and find me when you seek me with all
> your heart. I will be found by you," declares the LORD.
> (Jeremiah 29:11-14)

Do you have much of a sense yet of what God's plans for you might be? Write down what you know.

Ask God today for wisdom in balancing the expectations people have for you with those he has for you. Ask him for wisdom and insight and for courage to be obedient as you watch for the promised "hope and a future."

getting where you're going

2 Timothy 3:16-17

At fifteen, David had big plans for his life: He would make enough money to have a beautiful wife, three kids, and a summer vacation cottage on a lake. *Doctors make a lot of money,* he thought. *I guess I'll be a doctor.*

When David told the news about his career choice to his Uncle Marvin, who was a successful surgeon in a big-city hospital, Uncle Marvin took him seriously.

"That's wonderful, David. I think you've got the backbone and stamina to make it too. It's quite a grueling system, you know."

David didn't know, so he asked. Uncle Marvin explained that to become a doctor he would have to go to college for four years and then to medical school for another four years after that. Then followed a difficult period of residency.

David's face looked so dejected by the time Uncle Marvin had finished describing the life of a medical student that Uncle Marvin had to laugh. "Well, David, to get where you're going takes a lot of preparation and commitment."

What's Your Goal?

Do you already have in mind some possible directions for your future career? List your ideas here. (Dream big!) Put a check mark beside your number-one career choice.

What education, training, or other preparation does your number-one career choice require?

One Step at a Time

Perhaps David was too quick to get discouraged about the preparation a doctor must undergo. The average person's working life lasts for decades. Are a few years of training for a profession really so bad in comparison to that?

Besides, nowadays most people change jobs—and even careers—several times during their working life. Knowing how God has wired you and being willing to learn new skills along the way are more important qualities than ever.

How can you begin now to investigate career possibilities? (Ideas: take an interest survey, ask adults in your life what they think you'd be good at, spend a day with someone who has a job you're interested in.)

Tool of the Trade

As Christians, our number-one goal is to serve Christ in whatever we do. That may mean you'll serve God as an astronaut, a chef in a deli, a computer technician, a pro wrestler, a writer, a state governor, a painter, or something else. But whatever career God leads you into, you need to be equipped to serve him.

> All Scripture is inspired by God and is useful to teach
> us what is true and to make us realize what is wrong in
> our lives. It straightens us out and teaches us to do
> what is right. It is God's way of preparing us in every
> way, fully equipped for every good thing God wants us
> to do. (2 Timothy 3:16-17, NLT)

Work hard so God can approve you. Be a good worker,
one who does not need to be ashamed and who correctly
explains the word of truth. (2 Timothy 2:15, NLT)

Ask God to give you wisdom in planning your future. Commit yourself
to digging into his Word so that you may be "fully equipped for every
good thing."

one day at a time

Galatians 6:8-9

Jessica rubbed her eyes and turned off the sewing machine. She was sick to death of pins and needles, spools and bobbins, seams and hems. Why, oh, *why*, had she made that foolish promise?

When Jessica picked out the dress of her dreams for the Christmas banquet, her mom hit the ceiling when she saw the price on the tag. "No way, honey. Absolutely not."

They looked at others, but none of them came near that dress for style and originality, and none would look as perfect on Jessica. By the time they'd given up shopping, both Jessica and her mom were tired and grumpy.

Then a light bulb went on in Jessica's head. "Hey, Mom, what if I could have that dress for half price? Would you buy it for me then?"

Her mom laughed. "It's no good wishing. You won't find it for half price. But yes, I would."

"If you'll buy the pattern and material and everything, I'll make that dress myself!"

Jessica was a great seamstress. She'd started in home ec at school and gotten hooked. She often made clothes for herself, although the Christmas dress was the biggest challenge she'd yet tackled. She found a similar pattern and some beautiful material and got busy. Three weeks into the project, she still wasn't halfway finished, and she was getting tired of the whole mess.

Her mother had some good advice for her. "Jessica, just take it one day at a time—a sleeve today, a hem tomorrow, a zipper next Tuesday. You'll get there!"

That's Life!

Life is like that. When the initial enthusiasm over something wears off, and the end is not in sight, and your body and spirit are worn-out, it's easy to be discouraged. It can be like that in our relationship with God sometimes too.

 When you first came to know Christ, how did you feel? Describe that time or another time in your Christian life when you were on a "spiritual high."

🌀 Have you ever had a time when all your efforts seemed to add up to nothing? Describe a spiritually low time.

🌀 How would you describe the temperature of your enthusiasm for serving God right now—hot, cold, or lukewarm?

Hang In There!

When you became a Christian, you gave your life to the Lord. Sometimes it's hard to work for him and his kingdom when you don't see immediate results or when you're exhausted or when it seems like his promises are delayed. Hang in there! Our God's promises are true.

No matter how many promises God has made, they are "Yes" in Christ. (2 Corinthians 1:20)

The one who sows to please the Spirit, from the Spirit
will reap eternal life. Let us not become weary in doing
good, for at the proper time we will reap a harvest if we
do not give up. (Galatians 6:8-9)

Ask God to help you trust in his faithfulness. Commit yourself to serving
him one day at a time as you wait for the "harvest" he promises.

palaces and pearly gates

Revelation 22:5

When I was a little girl, my brothers and sisters and I were banned from Mom and Dad's room for more than a month before Christmas. The door was locked and Dad patrolled the hallway to keep us away from the door—where we could listen or try to sneak a peek—and out of Mom's hair.

On Christmas morning there appeared in our living room a beautiful, golden palace. It was bigger than any dollhouse I'd ever seen, and it had turrets and velvet draperies and jeweled walls and patterned floors.

We thought it was great. Our friends didn't have palaces in their living rooms, we were sure. It was our very own castle, handmade by Mom, and we were thrilled.

Treasure Hunt

What do you dream heaven will be like? Do you envision golden palaces? particular colors? Describe your imaginings.

In Revelation 21–22, the last pages of your Bible, the apostle John told of his vision of the heavenly city. Just for fun, do a treasure hunt of these two chapters, writing down all the beautiful things describing heaven that you can find.

A Forever Home

When I imagine heaven, the most vivid, overwhelming feature is *light*. There are sound biblical reasons for thinking of heaven in terms of light.

> There will be no more night. They will not need the
> light of a lamp or the light of the sun, for the Lord
> God will give them light. (Revelation 22:5)

The strongest feeling I have about heaven is a feeling of *home*. Living here in the world God created is often wonderful, but I'm looking forward to living in his perfect world, where he is.

Before leaving earth, Jesus gave an assurance that he's making a place in heaven for all his followers.

> In my Father's house are many rooms; if it were not so,
> I would have told you. I am going there to prepare a
> place for you. And if I go and prepare a place for you, I

will come back and take you to be with me that you
also may be where I am. (John 14:2-3)

This world is not our home; we are looking forward to
our city in heaven, which is yet to come. (Hebrews
13:14, NLT)

Get excited about your home in heaven with God! It could change the
way you live each day here on earth while you wait for the day you'll be
home forever.

keeping house

Matthew 16:27

Maria and Pablo had made it! For the first time in the history of their fifteen and sixteen years, their parents had left them alone for four days and
three nights. Dad had to fly to Hawaii for a sales conference and he'd
talked Mom into going along—sort of a second honeymoon. Pablo and
Maria had urged their mom to go too. They thought it would be a blast
to have the house to themselves.

And it *was* pretty fun—despite their bloopers cooking dinner, Pablo
locking them both out of the house, and squabbles over who had to
change the cat litter (Mom always did it).

The day their parents were due back, they pitched in together to get
the house cleaned up (okay, they'd let things slide just a little). They sorted
the stacks of mail, did three loads of laundry, vacuumed the living room,
scrubbed the bathroom, and attacked the pile of dirty dishes in the
kitchen.

Everything was ready by the time their parents arrived. Maria and
Pablo acted as if it were nothing when Mom went on and on about the

clean house and Dad congratulated them for their "responsibility." Best of all, Mom and Dad had brought them each a reward: a surfing poster and Waikiki T-shirt for Pablo, and tiny opal earrings for Maria.

Good Job, Guys!

Jesus told a story about a man who went on a trip, leaving his three servants in charge. Two of them did a good job with the responsibilities the master had given them, and this is what the boss said to them when he came home:

> Well done, good and faithful servant! You have been faithful with a few things; I will put you in charge of many things. Come and share your master's happiness! (Matthew 25:21)

But one servant wasted his time and his master's money because he was lazy and cowardly.

His boss said,

> You wicked, lazy servant!... You should have put my money on deposit with the bankers...
>   Throw that worthless servant outside, into the darkness, where there will be weeping and gnashing of teeth. (Matthew 25:26,27,30)

That last part is kind of brutal, isn't it? It's a reminder of how important being responsible to God really is.

Measuring Up

Have you ever been in a situation where you were given a great deal of responsibility? How did you handle it?

What can you do to earn a reputation for being responsible?

According to What You Have Done

Over and over, the Bible teaches that God rewards people according to what they have done.

> The Son of Man is going to come in his Father's glory
> with his angels, and then he will reward each person
> according to what he has done. (Matthew 16:27)

> Without faith it is impossible to please God, because
> anyone who comes to him must believe that he exists
> and that he rewards those who earnestly seek him.
> (Hebrews 11:6)

When the Chief Shepherd appears, you will receive the crown of glory that will never fade away. (1 Peter 5:4)

Remember who your Master is and what you're working for. Thank God in advance for the crown of glory that is waiting for you.

when i grow up

1 John 3:1-2

"What are you going to be when you grow up, dear?" Great-aunt Agatha beamed down at Ashley expectantly.

Ashley was sick of that question. When she was little, she'd wanted to be a farmer. Then for a while she wanted to be a nurse—a detective nurse. Then she went through a modeling stage; she envisioned herself with perfect face, hair, and body, walking gracefully down a runway in gorgeous and unusual clothes. But reality set in, and she went through a long string of other ideas: flight attendant, chef, interior designer, cosmetologist.

Most recently she'd been thinking about being an anthropologist-archaeologist. But she really didn't feel like telling her great-aunt about her dreams of making important discoveries about life in Bible times.

"I'm not sure, Aunt Agatha—maybe president!" she said.

Sneak Preview

When you imagine the future, how do you see yourself? What kind of an adult are you? Do you work? Are you balding

or gray-haired? How do you feel about young people? If you
are a parent, how do you treat your kids?

Still imagining your future, how do you see your spiritual life?
What are you doing to nurture your relationship with God?
What level of spiritual maturity have you achieved?

One Thing's for Sure

Only God knows the future, and we have some pretty wonderful clues in
his Word about what we will be like. Read the following scriptures, then
answer the questions.

How great is the love the Father has lavished on us, that
we should be called children of God!... Dear friends,
now we are children of God, and what we will be has
not yet been made known. But we know that when he
appears, we shall be like him, for we shall see him as he
is. (1 John 3:1-2)

To him who is able to keep you from falling and to
present you before his glorious presence without fault
and with great joy—to the only God our Savior be
glory, majesty, power and authority, through Jesus
Christ our Lord, before all ages, now and forevermore!
Amen. (Jude 24)

🌐 Whose child are you?

🌐 Who will you be like in the future?

🌐 How will you be presented before God?

Only one thing's for sure: We're going to be like Jesus when we finally get home to heaven. What could be more wonderful than being part of God's family? Ask God today to "keep you from falling." Thank him for his precious promises to you.

A freelance writer and editor, Annette LaPlaca has written for publications such as *Marriage Partnership* and *Today's Christian Woman*. She and her husband, David, live in the Chicago area and have three children.

New from
ASH MUNDAE

Available wherever you buy the music you love.

Hey, don't stop now.

If you really liked reading this devotional you may be interested to know that three more are available in the Red Hill Devos line. Written about you and for you, these books help you cope with life, friendships...maybe even long lines at the movies!

OTHER TITLES INCLUDE:

My Own Monster: A Youth Devotional on Friendship
    by Jeff and Ramona Tucker with foreword by Katy Hudson
This Thing Called Life: A Youth Devotional on Finding Direction
    by Jeff and Ramona Tucker with foreword by The Echoing Green
Forget Me Not: A Youth Devotional on Love and Dating
    by Mike Worley with foreword by Aurora

Real Devotions for Real Teens
from Shaw Books

Printed in the United States
by Baker & Taylor Publisher Services